Women or Men – Who Are the Victims?

=

Women or Men – Who Are the Victims?

Erin Pizzey
J.R. Shackleton
Peter Urwin

CIVITAS: Institute for the Study of Civil Society
London

First published December 2000

CIVITAS: Institute for the Study of Civil Society
The Mezzanine, Elizabeth House
39 York Road
London SE1 7NQ

'From the Personal to the Political' © Erin Pizzey

All other material

© Institute for the Study of Civil Society 2000
email: books@civitas.org.uk

ISBN 1-903 386-09 8

Typeset by CIVITAS
in New Century Schoolbook

Printed in Great Britain by
The Cromwell Press
Trowbridge, Wiltshire

Contents

The Authors

Erin Pizzey founded the first refuge for battered women and children in Chiswick in 1971. The importance of her work was immediately recognised and she became the founder of an international movement to provide shelter for victims of domestic violence. She has received numerous awards in recognition of her pioneering work. Her book *Scream Quietly or the Neighbours Will Hear* (1974) was the first book to deal with domestic violence. Her subsequent career as an author has embraced fiction, in the form of novels, short stories, poetry and plays, as well as books on domestic violence and a volume of early autobiography, *Infernal Child*. She has written and lectured widely on domestic violence, having completed two world-wide lecture tours, as well as testifying before the Attorney General's Task Force on Family Violence in Texas in 1984. Television programmes have included 'Sanctuary' in Channel 4's Cutting Edge series, and 'Who's Failing the Family?' in BBC2's Counterblast series in 1999.

J.R. Shackleton is Professor of Economics and Head of Westminster Business School. Educated at King's College Cambridge and the School of Oriental and African Studies, he previously lectured at Queen Mary College and was an economic adviser at the Department of Social Security. He has an extensive academic publications record and has written for think-tanks such as the Employment Policy Institute, the Institute of Economic Affairs and the Adam Smith Institute. He has frequently appeared on radio and television.

Peter Urwin is principal lecturer in economics at the University of Westminster. He has written on a variety of labour-market subjects, including discrimination, atypical employment, unemployment and the London labour market. He is a member of the University's Education, Training and the Labour Market Research Group and Director of the WBS Graduate Summer School. In his work with the London Chamber of Commerce and Industry he has helped to establish the *London Labour Market Briefings*. He is at present working on a number of projects including an analysis of the first employment destinations of Westminster students, an analysis of the incidence of training and education amongst older workers and a paper on over-education in the UK. He has taught on a wide range of courses in the fields of economics, business and management, with a present focus on the area of quantitative methods.

Foreword

Erin Pizzey became famous in the 1970s as the founder of a refuge for women escaping from their violent male partners. Initially she was embraced by the ultra-feminists of that time, but when she pointed out in a public lecture that 62 of the first 100 women who came into the refuge were as violent as the men they had left, she was denounced. Erin Pizzey had taken her stand against violence and in favour of justice for all, but she found that the ultra-feminists did not aspire to equal justice.

Her essay is a powerful, autobiographical tale of how a movement which initially sought fair treatment for all was captured by extremists who wanted preferments for the few. The strategy of ultra-feminists was to define women as a victim group oppressed by men. But for the strategy to succeed, no exceptions could be admitted and, consequently, any evidence which called into question the victim status of women had to be suppressed. Erin Pizzey's account shows, not only how evidence of female violence was disregarded, but also how the prevalence of female child abuse has been neglected.

Ultra-feminists sought victim status because it is a politically useful means of gaining preferential treatment and, perhaps, cash compensation. Throughout history there have always been groups seeking to turn the powers of government to their own advantage. Today, they frequently call for 'rights', but preferential public policies should be sharply distinguished from the traditional universal rights which give everyone a chance of success; the rights demanded by self-defined victim groups are better understood as legally sanctioned privileges which have more in common with the preferments awarded by pre-democracy monarchs to their favourites.

The modern strategy of turning victim status into a source of political power was perfected in America, initially by the self-appointed (often white) champions of black Americans and only later by ultra-feminists. In 1981 George Gilder observed that around 70 per cent of Americans—possessing some three-quarters of the national wealth—belonged to a victim group.[1] The trend was probably at its height in the early 1990s when another American scholar calculated that 374 per cent of Americans considered themselves to be members of one overlapping victim group or another.[2] Black Americans are a prime example of a real victim group which has suffered harsh discrimination. However, there is a difference between the modern 'power victim' and a 'real victim'. Today's 'power victims' are not asking for a fair chance under rules which apply equally to all; they demand legal reforms to give them an advantage at the expense of other people.

Because the strategy rests on winning acceptance for the belief that the group has been the victim of a wrong, then a group which has suffered no real wrong has to invent a grievance. One of the most successful ploys has been to apply the doctrine of 'proportional representation'. It asserts that if a group comprises a particular percentage of the total population, then it should also comprise the same proportion of every sub-division of the population, including occupations, institutions such as universities and prisons, or job categories such as chief executives. If the proportion of a group in any sub-division differs from that in the general population, it is assumed to be the result of discrimination by the oppressor group—men in the case of women, and whites where blacks are disproportionately represented.

Larry Elder, the black American author of *Ten Things You Can't Say in America*,[3] has coined the term 'victicrats' for groups who blame all their ills, problems and concerns on other people. Such claims to victim status have now become a leading rationale for political power, so much so that we are already well on the way to transforming our democracy (rule by *all* the people) into a 'victocracy' in which well-organised victim groups are able to determine the direction of public policy. Larry Elder has in mind black activists who exaggerate racial discrimination but the same phenomenon can be found among ultra-feminists who seek preferential treatment for women in the workplace.

Professor Shackleton and Peter Urwin, both from the University of Westminster, show how this doctrine has been applied in employment. The main technique has been to compare the average hourly rate of pay for all men with the average for all women. In 1998 the rate for women was 75 per cent of the rate for men. When allowance has been made for age, qualifications and years of work experience there is still an unexplained gap and, in keeping with classic victicrat strategy, anything unexplained is attributed to discrimination.

However, Professor Shackleton and Peter Urwin find this analysis defective when subjected to a more objective appraisal. In particular, a major part of the difference is explained by personal choices to marry and have children. For example, if the earnings of *single* men and *single* women with equivalent qualifications are compared, they are found to be similar. Moreover, single men earn *less* than married men, in part because the additional responsibilities borne by married men seem to encourage them to work harder. When *single* women are compared to *married* women the gradient is reversed, almost certainly because married women have decided to give priority to their children at the expense of work. In addition, many women choose occupations which allow them to take time off while their children are young and then to return to the workforce when they are older, such as secretarial and clerical work. To make these facts fit a theory which insists that women are entirely the victims of discrimination by men is more than a little difficult.

Furthermore, theories which focus on pay and qualifications disregard the disadvantages borne by men. According to Shackleton and Urwin, unemployment for men is higher than for women; they are more at risk of redundancy; they experience more injuries at work because they are over-represented in dangerous occupations; and they receive a lower return on their pension contributions. Higher earnings can be seen as a recognition by employers of these risks and disadvantages. Again, to make these facts fit a theory which insists that men are the oppressors and women the victims of discrimination would be difficult for any objective scholar. However, no such scruples seem to trouble the Equal Opportunities Commission and its allies.

The study by Professor Shackleton and Peter Urwin is in the tradition pioneered by Thomas Sowell in a series of books published since the early 1980s. In these studies, including *Markets and Minorities*,[4] *Civil Rights: Rhetoric or Reality*,[5] and *Preferential Policies: An International Perspective*,[6] he dissected and demolished the exaggerated and inaccurate claims of discrimination which had been built on the false doctrine of proportional representation.

Both the essays in this volume show how truth becomes an early casualty in the victim wars. Pizzey was a campaigner who set out to help real victims, whether they were men or women. This impartial concern was not acceptable to the victicrats. They were intent on gaining power and their case had to rest on the identification of women as the victims of an oppressor: men. So it is with 'discrimination' in the workplace. It is not permissible to argue that many women think motherhood is more important than work and that their personal choice explains much of the income disparity. Instead, women must be defined as the victims of oppression by (male) employers.

The challenge is to frame laws which give everyone who makes the effort a chance of success. In America, where quota-feminism first took root, many women have grown tired of being classified as if they were a downtrodden minority. Many have succeeded in business and the professions entirely on their own merits. Quota-feminism diminishes their achievement and such women are increasingly the most vocal opponents of continued policies of affirmative action. But no one seems to have told the British Government that women have moved on.

The enduring aim of CIVITAS' studies is to discover the legal, institutional and cultural framework most compatible with a free and democratic society. These essays demonstrate that the group animosity encouraged by the new victicrats can never be consistent with an equitable social order.

David G. Green

Men and the Labour Market

J.R. Shackleton and Peter Urwin

Introduction

People often view labour markets as 'unfair' environ-
ments, which treat different people in very unequal
ways. Some individuals are paid much more than others,
have greater access to jobs and better chances of promo-
tion. Of course most people probably accept the need for
some differentiation in pay in order to incentivise work
and reward effort. They also think it reasonable that more
highly-skilled and trained people should have priority
when firms are hiring, and be paid more than the un-
skilled and uneducated. Despite this, whenever a definable
group of people appears to suffer a common disadvantage,
their treatment is attacked as discriminatory. Some
groups may indeed have a claim for redress with which
many feel sympathy, but a lack of understanding of the
underlying processes of the labour market can lead to a
multiplication of such claims almost without limit.

Consider the following observations. Many ethnic
minority groups are paid less on average, and suffer
higher unemployment, than white workers. People with
disabilities find it harder than other people to get jobs.
Older workers are more often made redundant than prime-
age workers, and are less likely to get the chance to return

Material from the Labour Force Survey made available
through the Office of National Statistics and the ESRC Data
Archive has been used by permission of the Controller of
H.M. Stationery Office.

1

to work. Young workers are more often working in inse-
cure temporary jobs than more mature workers. Married
men earn more than single men. People in white-collar
jobs are more likely to have training paid for them than
manual workers. All these 'disadvantaged' groups are
likely to be vocal in their complaints, and the widespread
availability of labour-market data, particularly in the UK,
gives plenty of grist to their mill.

By far the most discussed dimension of labour-market
inequality, however, remains that between men and
women. The main outlines of gender inequality are
familiar.[1] In 1998 women's average hourly pay in this
country was about 75 per cent of that of men. Women are
concentrated in less well-paid occupational categories[2] and
a large proportion of their employment (over 40 per cent)
is part-time: part-time work is typically paid relatively
poorly. They are much less likely to be in senior management positions: one calculation is that only 14 per cent of
top managers are women although almost half the workforce is female.[3]

We do not dispute any of this, but it needs to be put into
a wider, dynamic, context. We argue, first, that women's
position in the labour market has improved considerably
in recent decades and is set, on current trends, to improve
still further while men's may be weakening. Second, we
point out that only a part of the labour-market advantage
apparently enjoyed by men can be attributed to discrimination in any sense which can be addressed by public
policy. Third, we point out some of the less obvious ways in
which *men* may be disadvantaged in the UK labour
market, and draw attention to particular groups of the
male workforce whose position is weak and deteriorating.

The Changing Picture

A snapshot picture of the apparent labour-market advantage of males should not be seen in isolation. Men's

dominance is weakening, and the position of women is strengthening, in a number of ways.

The Pay Gap is Narrowing

Women may only earn 75 per cent of men's hourly rate, but this proportion has risen steadily since the 1970s; 25 years ago the figure was only 62 per cent. Moreover, if we concentrate on full-time employees only, the proportion has risen from 60 per cent in the mid-1970s to 80 per cent in 1998.[4] In the younger age-groups the gap has narrowed even further. And, as we can see from Figure 1 (p. 4), the ratio is markedly higher than the average in some areas—notably the key area of professional occupations, where women earn over 90 per cent of men's hourly rates.[5]

Another indicator of the changing balance of power in the labour market is the proportion of women who earn hourly wages higher than those of their (working) partner. Labour Force Survey data show that in the early 1970s only around eight per cent of women were in this position; the figure is about one quarter today. Amongst women in full-time employment the figure is nearly 30 per cent.[6]

Men are a Declining Proportion of the Workforce

The proportion of women of working age who are economically active has risen considerably over the last quarter of a century. Women have fewer children; those they have are born to older mothers than previously, and women are much more likely to return to work while their children are still young. Thus, while in the mid-1970s only around 60 per cent of all women of working age were in work or looking for work, the figure today is around 70 per cent and seems set to rise further. By contrast, men's labour-market participation has declined. In 1975 over 97 per cent of men aged 16-64 were economically active, but by 1998 this figure had fallen to around 87 per cent. The decline in participation rates was particularly marked amongst older men, as we shall argue later.

4

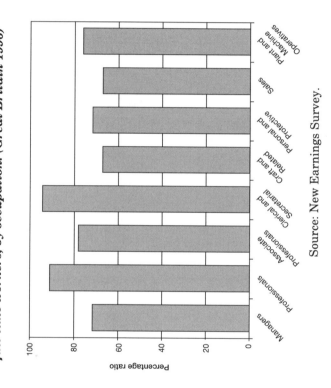

Figure 1
Percentage ratio of average female to male hourly earnings,
full-time workers, by occupation. (Great Britain 1996)

Source: New Earnings Survey.

These contrasting trends mean that men form a declining proportion of the workforce. Indeed, some predictions are that the number of female employees will exceed that of males early in the twenty-first century (although, since the self-employed are predominantly male, men will still remain the majority in the workforce as a whole).

The Changing Structure of Employment

The UK economy has undergone significant changes over the last quarter of a century, and this has had a major impact on the structure of employment. One notable feature has been the reduction in the proportion of employment accounted for by manufacturing, which fell from 31.5 per cent in 1979 to 20 per cent in 1994, and is projected to fall to just 14 per cent by 2006. At the same time, service sector employment has been rising and is expected to reach 49 per cent by 2006. These structural changes have been the result of a number of factors[7] and seem to have affected the employment fortunes of men and women in different ways. This is because men are concentrated in declining sectors such as manufacturing, mining and quarrying whereas women are more likely to be in expanding service areas such as education, health and personal services.[8]

Another aspect of structural change is that the share of part-time work in total employment has risen over time. Employers have sought greater flexibility, particularly in relation to weekend working in retailing and other expanding service fields. These extra part-time jobs have overwhelmingly gone to females: men continue to be a small minority amongst part-timers.

Women at the Top

Traditional male dominance amongst managers and professionals is increasingly under threat. Between 1981 and 1996 the number of managers and administrators in Britain increased by one-and-a-half million; women took

55 per cent of the extra jobs. Of 450,000 extra professional jobs created in the same period, women took 69 per cent.[9] In the younger age-groups, women are now approaching numerical parity with men in the higher occupations. Of course, leading positions in these occupational categories are, as indicated earlier, still dominated by men. But this is changing. As Table 1 (p. 7) shows, the proportion of senior managers who are women is steadily growing.

There is clearly a 'cohort' or generational effect here. The proportion of women who are chief executives is about the same as the proportion who were senior function heads a decade earlier.[10] Over time we would expect a growing proportion of women to reach through to top posts as there is now a larger pool of women with experience at lower levels of the management hierarchy.

Men are Falling Behind in Education and Training

The future prospects of the upcoming generations of men and women are going to be affected by the education and training they have received. Table 2 (p. 8) shows that the educational qualifications of both men and women improved dramatically from the mid-1970s to the mid-1990s. However, in the younger age-groups the improvement is significantly more marked for women than for men. Amongst those in employment aged 16-24, women have achieved virtual parity with men. A larger proportion of young men than young women has no educational achievements. This position will become even more apparent in the next few years. Currently a higher proportion of girls than boys achieve good GCSE results.[11]

Employability is enhanced by work-related training as well as educational qualifications. Women in all age-groups have for some years had a higher incidence of job-related training than that seen among men, with an approximate five percentage-point difference for each age-group. However industries and occupations where employment is dominated by women display a higher incidence of employer-provided training, so it is necessary to correct for

Table 1
Percentage of Management Positions Held by Women

Position	1989	1990	1991	1992	1993	1994	1995	1996	1997	1998
Chief/deputy chief executive	1.1	1.5	1.7	2.5	2.9	3.0	2.9	3.1	3.0	3.4
Other directors	2.5	3.6	4.3	4.4	6.5	5.6	5.6	5.8	6.9	7.0
Senior function head	3.4	4.3	5.5	6.5	7.5	6.3	6.5	6.9	7.4	8.3
Function head	6.4	7.4	8.2	8.9	9.6	9.3	9.1	10.3	10.7	12.5
Department manager	7.3	7.7	8.3	8.7	10.0	11.4	13.0	17.7	19.3	18.7
Section manager	10.6	12.1	12.7	11.6	13.5	14.4	16.3	17.4	13.4	16.1
Section leader	13.6	15.9	17.0	17.4	19.1	20.8	22.2	18.2	18.8	22.2
Total	**6.9**	**8.0**	**8.9**	**9.1**	**10.5**	**10.7**	**11.2**	**12.4**	**12.6**	**14.0**

Source: Desai, *et al.*, 'Gender and the labour market', in Gregg, P. and Wadsworth, J., *The State of Working Britain*, Manchester: Manchester University Press, 1999.

this to establish the effects of gender. Studies carried out on data from the 1980s[12] identified a higher incidence of training for men than for women during this period, once industrial and occupational concentration had been accounted for. However, as Green, Machin and Wilkinson[13] point out, this gender difference has largely disappeared in recent years, with women and men now exhibiting broadly similar training profiles. Recent unpublished work supports this analysis.[14]

Table 2
Highest Qualification Obtained for All in Employment

Aged 16-59	1974-1976		1993-1995	
	Men	Women	Men	Women
Degree	5.2	1.9	15.6	10.1
Higher intermediate	9.1	9.3	20.1	19.1
Lower intermediate	36.3	29.9	44.0	47.2
None	49.3	58.9	20.4	23.6
Aged 16-24				
Degree	2.6	1.7	6.8	6.4
Higher intermediate	10.6	10.6	18.7	19.3
Lower intermediate	51.0	53.4	63.3	65.9
None	35.7	34.2	11.2	8.4

Source: Desai, et al., 'Gender and the labour market', 1999.

Legislative Support for Women in Employment

In the last 30 years a steady stream of legislation and court judgements has improved the position of women in employment. Equal pay and sex discrimination laws in the 1970s, plus amendments to the Equal Pay Act in 1983, and maternity rights legislation in 1978 and 1993, with further extensions in 1999, have all been specifically aimed at improving women's position in the labour market. Other interventions have had a more general remit but are likely to have had a disproportionately favourable effect on women, for instance recent minimum wage legislation and the right to time off work to cope with family emergencies (government estimates suggest 35 per cent of women and only two per cent of men will take significant advantage of this right). Successive European Court judgments have extended rights or privileges enjoyed by full-time employees (for example in relation to pensions) to part-time employees, who remain disproportionately female. Incidentally, the extension of legislation to cover part-time workers contrasts with the position of another class of 'atypical' workers whose numbers have been growing significantly —the self-employed—but are predominantly male.

It is also worth noting that trade unions have had their powers severely reduced since the 1970s.[15] Unionised employees, disproportionately male, have typically enjoyed a pay mark-up in relation to non-unionised labour with similar qualifications and experience; this source of advantage is now available to a much smaller proportion of the male workforce.

Discrimination Against Women?

So the picture of male advantage in the labour market needs some qualification. Nevertheless there is no doubt that women, on average, earn significantly less than men when working similar hours in similar jobs. Is this evidence of employer discrimination?

Possibly. But to form a judgment we have to understand how labour markets work. Economists argue that, in a competitive labour market, individuals' pay will reflect their marginal productivity—what they add to the firm's output. Productivity will be affected by such factors as age, years of work-experience, academic and professional qualifications. Holding these variables constant, a pay differential between two groups *may* be attributable to discrimination. Many studies have found such a productivity-corrected differential between men and women and taken this 'gender gap' as evidence of discrimination. Strictly speaking, however, the residual differential is a measure of the researchers' inability to explain: important variables may have been omitted. Some of these variables may be unobservable differences in motivation.

One difference which has to be taken into account is the marital status of individuals. Marriage (or cohabitation) affects motivation and behaviour. So does the advent of children. This may be thought trivial, or involve acceptance of gendered family roles. But consider the situation of single men and married men with the same experience, qualification and so forth; it is a well-established empirical finding that the latter earn significantly more than the former.[16] A plausible hypothesis is that the acceptance of family responsibilities motivates men to work harder and earn more. There appears also to be a difference between single women and married women which works in the opposite direction; single women with given productivity characteristics earn more than married women with identical characteristics. What is particularly interesting is that there is only a small difference between the pay of single men and single women with the same productivity characteristics: Polachek and Siebert argue that the gap is often insignificant.

What emerges, then, is a more complicated picture than is often thought: married men with a particular set of productivity characteristics earn most; single women and single men earn roughly the same; married women earn least. Work on the effect of children by Joshi, Paci and Waldfogel adds yet more to the picture.[17] They find that the pay gap between men and childless women—whether married or single—is much smaller than that between men and women with children.

Another issue needs to be briefly mentioned: the possibility that men earn more than women because women are crowded into low-paying industries and occupations, whereas men's employment patterns are much more diverse. It is certainly true that women predominate in some occupations (clerical and secretarial, most obviously) and industries (hotels and restaurants, education and health). And some occupations and industries pay better than others: this will reflect factors such as the quantity of capital employed per worker, which affects underlying labour productivity. However, the variations in pay between industries and occupations does not statistically account for a large proportion of the gender pay gap. Moreover all jobs and occupations have some mix of men and women and it is unclear that there are major barriers to movement into particular work areas; labour-market segmentation is not a key feature of the UK labour market.

The implication of this discussion is that 'discrimination' may be a misleading description of the processes which produce inequality in the labour market. To the extent that decisions to marry and have children alter behaviour by both males and females, some pay inequalities will tend to emerge. Because women and men choose to enter different industries and occupations, again differences in average pay will result. Over time, changing patterns of behaviour will, of course, alter outcomes. In a controversial recent paper, Rowthorn has argued that easier, no-fault, divorce in the UK has led to women working more outside the home as an insurance against marital breakdown; this may have contributed to narrowing the gender pay-gap.[18]

The analysis here suggests that inequality between men and women at work is not easy to eradicate by penalising employers who are held to blame for the situation. Nor is there an obvious pay formula which would eradicate gender bias. The lecturers' union NATFHE has published a report[19] showing a considerable gap between men's and women's average pay in higher education. Universities were listed in order of the size of the relative differential. Interestingly, the institution with the largest gap was the London Business School, the only institution with a fully-developed performance-related pay system for lecturers. PRP systems are often held to discriminate against women. But all other universities are on incremental pay scales which have also been held to discriminate against women because they reward continuous tenure, which women are less likely to experience because of career breaks.

Men May Be Disadvantaged, Too

Most comparisons of men's and women's labour-market experience concentrate upon indicators, such as pay, which show men with an advantage. However Adam Smith, in his *Wealth of Nations*, long ago pointed out that pay tends to adjust to offset other characteristics of the job. Thus, other things being equal, more dangerous jobs are paid more than safe jobs; jobs for which individuals have to finance their own training have to be paid more highly to compensate; jobs which are irregular have to be paid more than those where employment is steady. There is an argument for saying that, despite their advantage in pay and some other employment characteristics, men's labour-market position in the UK has a definite downside.

Unemployment

Male unemployment in Britain, unlike other European countries, is significantly higher than female unemployment.[20] In summer 1999 the ILO measure of unemployment stood at 6.8 per cent for men as against only 5.6 per cent for women. The gap was even wider during the recession of the early 1990s, reaching a maximum of 5.9 percentage points in 1993.[21] It is worth noting that the differential is greatest for young people; in spring 1998

10.4 per cent of economically active young women aged 16-24 were unemployed, but so were 14.0 per cent of young men in the same age-group.

Redundancy

One factor influencing the inflow into unemployment is redundancy. In 1998 the redundancy rate for men was 11 per 1,000 employees, as against only seven per 1,000 for women.[22] This is partly the result of the employment pattern of men and women. Men are disproportionately employed in manufacturing (where redundancies ran at 15 per thousand in 1998) rather than services (seven per thousand). Women are over-represented in more secure employment in public administration, education and health, where redundancies ran at only two per 1,000 employees in 1998.

Part-time Work and Underemployment

Part-time employment has traditionally been associated with females. It is true that the proportion of men working part-time has grown steadily since the 1970s. However, much of this expansion has come from students. If we ignore students and those men who have chosen part-time work because of illness or disability, a significant minority of men working part-time wish to work full-time, as Table 3 (p. 14) illustrates. This suggests that a substantial number of male part-timers are underemployed. By contrast, the overwhelming majority of women part-time workers are working part-time because they do not want a full-time job. Moreover female part-timers routinely report themselves as more satisfied with their jobs than full-timers.[23]

Hours Worked

Despite the growth of part-time employment amongst males, men continue to work longer hours in the labour market than women. According to the Labour Force Survey, men in full-time employment worked an average of 39.3 'normal' hours per week in spring 1998. This was less than the 40.2 hours of normal work at a similar stage of the business cycle a decade previously. However paid overtime rose from 3.3 hours a week to 4.5 hours, while unpaid overtime increased from 1.8 hours to 3.2 hours over the period. Thus the total amount worked rose from 45.3 to 47.0 hours. Women in full-time employment also worked longer hours on average in 1998 than in 1988, the total rising from 40.0 to 43.0 hours. The rise in overall hours worked by women is accounted for by a large increase (from 1.4 hours to 4.0) in unpaid—and self-reported —overtime; normal hours have fallen and paid overtime has barely increased for women.

Table 3

Reasons for Choosing Part-time Employment as a Percentage of Males and Females Working Part-time

Sex	Student or at school	Ill or disabled	Could not find full-time job	Did not want full-time job
Male	40%	4%	26%	30%
Female	11%	1%	9%	78%

Source: *Labour Force Survey*, Spring 1998

Injuries

Longer hours may be associated with greater risk of injury. Certainly, another area where male employees are at a disadvantage is in relation to industrial injuries. The most dangerous occupations include plant and machinery operatives (79 per cent male), craft and related occupations (91 per cent). The most dangerous industries are transport and communications, energy and water, construction, manufacturing and agriculture and fishing. All these industries are disproportionate employers of men. It is not surprising, therefore, that in winter 1996-97 some 5.8 per cent of men reported a work-related injury in the last twelve months as against only 3.3 per cent of women. In the same period the more serious injuries reported under Health and Safety legislation were almost twice as common amongst men as amongst women.[24] Work-related deaths are also substantially more common amongst men.

Sickness Absence

Men in the workforce are as likely to suffer from a work-limiting disability as women.[25] However they are much less likely to have time off work for sickness than women. Labour Force Survey data for spring 1998 show that 3.8 per cent of males in full-time employment took any days of sickness absence in a given week compared with 5.6 per cent of females. Amongst part-time workers the figures were 4.0 and 4.6 per cent respectively. Apparently the gap between men and women has increased in the last quarter of a century.[26]

Pensions

It is well known that men live on average shorter lives than women, and typically retire later. This means that their expected period of retirement is much shorter. The state pension system, and most occupational schemes, are actuarially unfair to men. A man and woman with similar characteristics, retiring at the same age and on the same salary, can expect different benefits for the same contributions.

Compensating Differentials and Pay Inequality

The implication of the issues we have touched on in this section is that the picture of gender inequality which simply concentrates on pay differentials may be misleading. If men are paid more than women, but have (for example) higher risk of injury, less secure jobs and poorer returns on their pensions, they are suffering offsetting disadvantages which need to be taken into account in a fuller comparison.

Particular Disadvantaged Groups Of Men

If men's labour-market position generally has a downside which is rarely stressed in public debate, we can identify groups of men who are particularly disadvantaged. In this section we briefly discuss the position of some of the most obvious of these groups.

Young Men

We have seen that young males are doing relatively badly in the labour market as they are less qualified, less likely to receive training and more likely to be unemployed than their female equivalents.

Young men are much less likely to be married than they were in the past, and less likely to be in a stable relationship with a partner and a child. The average age of first parenthood has risen, as has the number of young women bringing up children on their own. In the United States, where this shift in behaviour has gone further than in the UK, it has been argued that it is associated with a prolongation of adolescent irresponsibility which has weakened the labour-market position of young men. George Akerlof has argued that single men have lower wages, are less likely to be in the workforce, more likely to be unemployed because they have quit their job, have higher unemployment rates and are less likely to have worked a full year, than their married counterparts.[27] Those with less stable labour-force attachment are also more likely to be both perpetrators and victims of crime and to be associated with drug or alcohol abuse.

A broadly similar picture could be painted in the UK, where there is a significant minority of young males whose behaviour and labour-market status is locked in a vicious circle from which it is difficult for individuals to extricate themselves. Although the current government's New Deal is aimed in part at this group, and its Social Exclusion Unit is looking at other ways to reintegrate disaffected young men, there is a considerable task ahead. Significant numbers—the highest in the European Union—have disappeared completely from official sight; they are not in education or employment, nor claiming benefit, nor on the electoral register. And the UK has one of the largest proportions of young men who are incarcerated in the developed world. Such young men (young women are rarely imprisoned) are often illiterate and lacking in skills, and are ill-equipped for any kind of job in 'straight' society.

The 'Detached Male Workforce'

It is not just *young* males who have dropped out of the workforce. Over the last two decades there has been a substantial decline in men's economic activity rate (the proportion in work or training or actively seeking work). This is found in all age-groups. Ignoring the youngest group, we find that the proportion of 20-24-year-old males who were economically inactive rose from 9.3 per cent to 16.6 per cent between 1977 and 1997; for 25-34-year-olds the rise was from 2.3 per cent to 6.6 per cent; for 35-49-year-olds from 2.3 per cent to 8.0 per cent. It is particularly significant that the proportion of all non-student men of working age with no formal qualifications who are economically inactive rose from just 4.9 per cent to 28.7 per cent over this period.[28]

In addition to those formally defined as inactive, there is a penumbra of other individuals with weak attachment to the workforce, for instance the long-term unemployed, those in part-time employment and men in receipt of various sickness or disability benefits. In their recent study, Beatty and Fothergill looked at all men aged 25-64 who had not had a regular full-time job for most or all of the preceding six months. This group they classified as the 'detached' male workforce. They point out that labour-market detachment amongst men is widespread, but that in particular parts of the country it is particularly common, reaching 30 per cent or more of the age-group even in the late 1990s.

Older Males and Early Retirement

The situation of older men in the workforce has received considerable attention recently.[29] Figure 2 (p. 19) shows that the decline in economic activity amongst older age-groups, often discussed with alarm in the context of the 'demographic time bomb', is essentially a male phenomenon. Between 1975 and 1985 the proportion of 55-64-year-old males who were economically active dropped dramatically. This was partly a voluntary movement, as older workers' improved pension position and levels of savings gave them greater choice. Much of it, however, was the consequence of recession and restructuring in that period. Since the mid-1980s the decline in activity amongst older men has slowed, but there has been no reversion to the levels of labour-force participation which prevailed before the mid-1970s. Indeed, participation is expected to fall still further amongst older males during the first decade of the twenty-first century.[30]

For women the position has been rather different. Although there was a slight overall decline in older women's labour-force participation from the mid-70s to the mid-80s, this has since been reversed. Whilst this does reflect a relative fall in activity amongst older women in the UK,[31] this is less steep than that for older men. And over the next ten years older women's participation is expected to rise, especially amongst 60-64-year-olds, as the country moves towards equalisation of state pension age.

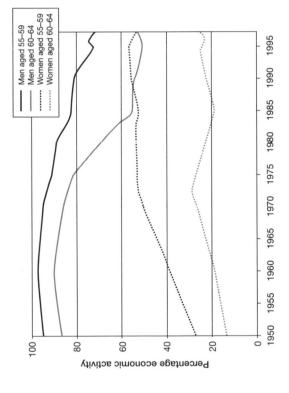

Figure 2
*Economic Activity Rates of Older Women and Men
in Great Britain, 1951-1997*

Men aged 55–59
Men aged 60–64
Women aged 55–59
Women aged 60–64

Percentage economic activity

1950 1955 1960 1965 1970 1975 1980 1985 1990 1995

100   80   60   40   20   0

Source: *Employment Gazette*, April 1995; *Labour Force Survey*, Spring 1995-97

To the extent that decline in older men's economic activity and labour-force attachment is involuntary (and Beatty and Fothergill, for instance, conclude that the voluntarily early retired are a minority amongst the 'detached' group), many older men may feel that they are being discriminated against on grounds of age. It has indeed been suggested that age discrimination should itself be made illegal, as is discrimination against women. So far, however, the government has set its face against a policy which would pose immense practical difficulties, even if it were thought desirable.

Ethnic Minority Males

We have already suggested that a picture of 'men' as a group doing better than 'women' as a group is considerably over-simplified. This position is strengthened when we look at the ethnic dimension of economic advantage. Black and Bangladeshi/Pakistani men are much less likely to be in employment than whites, Indians or Chinese. Table 4 (p. 21) shows that, of those with jobs, these groups do very badly in pay terms. It is useful to see how gender inequality does not map perfectly to ethnic inequality. The data show that white women have higher hourly average earnings than Pakistani/Bangladeshi men. A particularly significant comparison is that between black men and black women. Black men's hourly pay is well below that of black women.

Further disaggregation reveals sub-groups of ethnic minority men who are even more starkly disadvantaged. Thus young black men of Caribbean background are one of the worst-off groups of working age with very low average pay and an unemployment rate twice that of whites of the same age. Berthoud[32] pinpoints three weaknesses—poor educational qualifications, lack of family commitments (a larger proportion of young Caribbean men are unattached than any other group—and we have already seen how this affects labour-market behaviour) and lack of work experience. He takes a pessimistic view of the prospects of this group, arguing that there are no grounds for assuming that their disadvantage will disappear over time.

Table 4

Mean Real Hourly Wages by Ethnic Group in 1997

	White	Black	Indian	Pakistani and Bangladeshi	Mixed and other
All	7.54	7.03	7.41	5.59	7.81
Male	8.67	6.74	8.49	5.73	8.51
Female	6.34	7.32	6.01	5.18	7.05

Source: *Employment Audit, 1998.*

Conclusion

In this chapter we have tried to offer a rather different view of gender inequality in the labour market. While men on average 'do better' in the workplace than women, this kind of generalisation is less helpful than it might be. We have shown that women's position has improved significantly in the last quarter of a century, and can be expected to improve still further in the new century in the light of current trends in the economy, improved education and training and changes in social attitudes. Women are improving their position both absolutely and relative to men.

We have argued that much continuing inequality reflects 'choice' on the part of men and women, in terms of industries and occupations entered and decisions to marry and have children. To the extent that patterns of choice are altering, we would expect the pattern of gender pay differentials to alter. An implication, however, is that it may be mistaken to blame employers for labour-market outcomes and to use the law and public opinion to penalise firms whose pattern of pay and employment does not precisely match an idealised picture of equality.

We went on to point out that better pay for men may be offset to some extent by other less attractive features of employment, with the implication that discussions of the gender pay gap may need to be supplemented with a fuller analysis of employment conditions. Finally we highlighted a number of groups amongst the male working-age population who are doing very badly in the labour market—and indeed worse than a large proportion of the female workforce.

The overall conclusion which we draw is that the labour market is a very complicated place. There is pressure from politicians and interest groups to draw simplified messages from inequalities between broad groups such as men and women. If this is then translated into policy measures which penalise employers and broad categories of employees in the belief that a perceived inequality will then disappear, that expectation is likely to be confounded.

From the Personal to the Political

Erin Pizzey

What Is The Women's Movement For?

One of the most interesting debates in the new century might well be the question of how and why the women's movement in the Western world was founded. Did it, as many of the women journalists explained it, rise from the needs of the oppressed women of the world? Or was it manufactured by leftist women tired of being relegated to the role of 'chief-cook-and-bottle-washer' in the kitchens of their revolutionary lovers? According to Susan Brown-miller in her excellent history of the women's movement, *In Our Time: Memoir of a Revolution*,[1] the women's movement was founded in New York when many female activists returned from Mississippi after attempting to help black people register their votes. The men in the revolutionary movements, who expected them to take inferior roles, hugely discouraged the women activists. When Stokely Carmichael was asked about the position of women in the forthcoming revolution, he replied: 'What is the position of women in SNCC (Student Non-violent Co-ordinating Committee)? The position of women in SNCC is prone', thereby precipitating a revolution the outcome of which even the most dedicated of Black Panthers would be unable to imagine.

I joined this amorphous movement in 1971 when Jill Tweedie and other left-wing journalists were writing in newspapers and magazines of the needs of women and their very sensible demands. There was a sigh of relief from millions of women in Britain whose reading matter consisted of cooking and knitting patterns. With the exception of *She* magazine, which was run by the redoubtable lesbian Nancy Spain, most of us were lectured on how to be perfect housewives.

The *Guardian* gave details of how to contact this new, exciting, liberation movement for women, so I telephoned the main number in London and was directed to my local group in Chiswick. I left my husband facing his first night of babysitting the children and set off for my meeting. I was less than impressed to find myself in a very big house hosted by a small woman with a sharp tongue. If I thought I was going to join a movement that was going to lessen my isolation with my two small children I was wrong. 'Your problem is not your isolation,' I was told. 'Your problem is your husband, he oppresses you.' I looked at the other white middle-class women in the room with me and tried not to blush. We were also told that we were to call ourselves a collective, to refer to each other as 'comrades' and pay three pounds ten shillings to join the Women's Liberation Movement. There were posters of fierce women waving guns over their heads and a very large portrait of Chairman Mao on the wall. The violence of the posters upset me because I was a child born in 1939—a child born into a terrible war.

I was born in China where my father was working in the consular service. Both parents were friends of Chaing Kai Check who was exiled to Taiwan by the communists. My parents and my brother, who returned to China in 1942, were captured by the communists and put under house arrest for several years. My twin sister and myself believed them to be dead. My father's hatred and disgust for any totalitarian regime left its mark on me and I was offended by what I saw as a manipulative attempt by the local communist party to add my three pounds ten shillings to its account.

Still, I passionately believed that women in this country needed a place to meet and to organise in their local areas.

I was aware of a huge group of isolated women, many of whom had invaluable natural gifts and some work experience, that we could use in our own communities. I braved the hostility towards my high heels and my make-up in the women's liberation office and took over the typing.

I didn't last long. What I saw were groups of left-leaning, white, middle-class women gathering together to hate men. Their slogan was 'make the personal political'. I saw that the most vociferous and the most violent of the women took their own personal damage, their anger against their fathers, and expanded their rage to include all men. Many of these women were 'trust-fund bunnies', meaning that they lived off their rich fathers' money. What made the movement so immediately violent was the fact that it was founded in England by American women who were on the run from the FBI. This was not the first time America exported its revolutionaries: Trotsky had been deported along with other revolutionaries years before. Some went to Germany to join the Badermeinhof group. Others went to Holland to join the Red Stockings, and some chose to come to England. London seemed destined to become the revolutionary hotbed for terrorists from all over the world, Beirut-by-Thames. I was at a BBC party when the taxpayers shelled out to pay for all the famous revolutionaries to be flown in from across the world to make a BBC programme. I watched 'Danny The Red' argue with the producer for bigger expenses and a more comfortable hotel. Kenneth Tynan told me that we should take over the BBC and launch the revolution ourselves. I was also forced to attend a tedious lecture at which Bernadette Devlin harangued us and various Black Panthers gave salutes. A row of BBC would-be revolutionaries raised their pallid fists in reply. In 1970 terrorist women from groups everywhere poured into London for the first women's liberation march, but by this time I was becoming far more politically aware.

I stood up in many of the violent and threatening collectives to tell the leaders of this movement that hating all

men was not anything that I wanted to be part of. I told
them that I considered my life a luxury. I had a husband
who went to work and paid the mortgage so that I could
stay home with my two children. I reminded them that
most people were slaves. I reminded them of the murder-
ous regimes of Mao and of Stalin, but of course many of
those women were followers of both Mao and Stalin. (We
discover, thanks to Mike Horowitz's interesting book
Hating Whitey and Other Progressive Causes,[2] that Betty
Friedan was a Stalinist Marxist.) Their attitude was that,
if 30 million died for the cause of the revolution, so be it. I
was hated with a passion and finally, ironically, excluded
from the liberation movement.

The Beginning Of The Women's Refuge Movement —And Its Capture

I left to open a small community centre for women and
their children where I would try to realise my vision of
lessening the isolation found in the Western world due to
the breaking down of the extended family. For many
months this little community centre for women and their
children attracted all sorts of women eager to have a place
where they could use their abilities and entertain their
children. Very soon women who avoided the statutory
services came to us and we befriended them. Then one day
a woman came in to the little upstairs office and took off
her jersey. Her body was streaked with black and purple
bruising. 'My husband beats me,' she said. I took her home
that night rather than leave her on her own. However,
from the very beginning I was aware of the violence of
some of the women coming into my refuge. By this time I
had attracted the two things the women's movement
wanted: a just cause to clothe their political agenda and
money to fund this agenda. By 1972 the women's movement had run out of money. Ordinary English women were
far too intelligent and educated to want to be included in
a movement that so obviously desired to destroy the family

and men. Only very isolated pockets of women living in areas like Islington and Kew refused to let their boy-children have any male toys, and boasted that their husbands or lovers had now been changed overnight into 'new men'. The rest of us accepted that men would always be men and any help in the house was gratefully accepted.

While the bra-burning antics of the women's movement became a stock joke of newspapers and television comedians, the movement slid into obscurity, except in certain newspapers and in the academic circles. Here the misandry of the women's movement found its exponents amongst untenured women professors. They created a whole new discipline called 'women's studies' to brainwash generations of young women coming into universities.

I found schools filled with 'teachers' who were not teachers but political activists. I went to universities to lecture and was roundly berated when I pointed out that 62 of the first 100 women who came into the refuge were as violent as the men they left. I addressed public meetings and talked about 'battered men'. Since domestic violence was considered a female issue it was women journalists who covered the subject. If I tried to interest newspapers in publishing my views I came up again the same problem. I was in the hands of women editors who refused to allow me to air my views. Things were no better in the publishing field: editors routinely censor books, especially the radical lesbian editors. There was, and still is, strict censorship of anyone trying to break the code of silence. No one wants to acknowledge the extent of the damage that the feminist movement has done to the family and to men in the last 30 years.

Over that period I have seen great corruption in the English courts. I have seen fathers of children denied their rights and persecuted. I have seen our own government concur with a television advertisement on Scottish television in which children were advised to ring a telephone number should their fathers shout at their mothers. I had a very early memory of a small girl of my own age who also lived in China during the time of the communist take-over, denouncing her father who was taken from the family and tortured for seven years. I watched as 'consciousness-raising groups', which again reminded me of Mao's teachings, spread like a rash over the Western world, designed to brain-wash women into believing that their husbands were the enemy and must be eradicated from the family. I saw the rise of the single mother glorified in the women's sections of some newspapers. Four women journalists wrote about their search for the right man to give them their children and the four women promised their readers that the children would never even know their fathers. I felt that these rich, privileged women journalists were acting irresponsibly, for by now I was divorced from my husband and, as a single mother, I suffered the anxiety and the loneliness of bringing up children on my own.

Most of all I saw feminist women teachers discriminate against the boys in their classrooms. I saw the huge tide of women pouring into the workforce hungry for jobs and careers. Many had no choice. Financial hardship made it imperative for both partners to work. In spite of promises, there was no national childcare plan, so illegal and often dangerous attempts were made by other women to take in children. Men, freed from any restraint by the birth-control pill, demanded sex whenever they wanted it, and then many ran away from the subsequent pregnancies. London became not only the abortion capital of the world but also had the highest level of teenage births in the West. Men turned their backs on marriage and commitment, with many fearing, quite rightly, that whatever commitment they offered would end up with women fleecing them for the rest of their lives.

Ostracism Around The Globe

In 1977 Congresswoman Lindy Boggs and Congressman Newton-Steer invited me to a luncheon of honour on

Capitol Hill. I realised by now that what I was going to say
would make me deeply unpopular. Everyone who came to
meet me always assumed quite wrongly that I was a
'feminist'. I was nothing of the sort. I have always disbe-
lieved in 'ists' of any sort and the only way I am willing to
define myself is as 'a lover of God in all his aspects'. By the
end of my speech everyone at the table was avoiding me,
and I fared no better at the Press Club in Washington. The
expression on the faces of the hard-bitten women journalists was a source of amusement to me. Many of my speaking engagements were cancelled, especially in New York
and Boston. I spent a hilarious night with another member
of staff in a communal lesbian household of professors in
Anne Arbor, but I was very glad indeed to be hosted in
another city by a sweet young wife and mother. I could see
then that the feminist movement everywhere had hi-
jacked the whole issue of domestic violence to fulfil their
political ambitions and to fill their pockets. By now
feminists in America and other countries were redrafting
the law.

> In the past decade, feminist legal theory has become a formidable
> presence in many of America's top law schools. Feminist activism
> has also had a major impact on many areas of the law, including
> rape, self-defence, domestic violence, and such new legal categories
> as sexual harassment. However, the ideology of legal feminism
> today goes far beyond the original and widely supported goal of
> equal treatment for both sexes. The new agenda is to redistribute
> power from the 'dominant class' (men) to the 'subordinate class'
> (women), and such key concepts of Western jurisprudence as
> judicial neutrality and individual rights are declared to be
> patriarchal fictions designed to protect male privilege.[3]

My sojourn in Germany at the invitation of the German
minister for sport was no different. I left some very grim-
looking German refuge-workers at a dinner table because
I could no longer bear the future of what the refuges were
to become. I watched the feminist movement build its
bastions of hatred against men, fortresses where women
were to be taught that all men were rapists and bastards,

and I witnessed the damage done to the children in the refuges who were taught that men were not to be trusted.

I was asked to visit New Zealand in 1978 and I had hoped to be invited to speak to groups involved with refuges in Australia. At that time New Zealand had not yet fallen into the arms of the totalitarian women's movement (it has now), but I was denied a visit to Australia because the militant lesbian movement there had control of most of the refuges. Since, as in many other countries, the lesbian movement was in control of most of the financing, they merely instructed the Australian refuges to withdraw their invitations.

To show how this movement had the power to censor information, I will quote one example amongst many. In 1984 I gave evidence in San Antonio to the Texas Task Force on Family Violence. There was huge trepidation in the minds of the various shelter groups who were gathered there to give their testimony. Woman after woman gave her personal evidence. In some cases the evidence was grim and dreadful. They were the genuine victims of their partner's violence. However, many of the women giving evidence gave a bravura performance which elicited much clapping from the audience of excitable sisters but puzzled the members of the Attorney General's Task Force. 'I understand your grief', one of the women members said to a particularly histrionic woman, 'but you said this happened to you ten years ago. Don't you think it is time you moved on?' She spoke for most of her task force who were very puzzled by what they could see as a definite split between the women who were genuinely giving evidence and the others who were violence-prone women who were not innocent victims of their partner's violence. I gave my evidence about the differences between women who were genuine battered women and those who were violent themselves and needed treatment. The committee thanked me and I received a standing ovation from the audience. When the report arrived at my home in Santa Fe, it recorded one meaningless sentence and referred to me as 'Erin Shapiro, author', even though my written evidence was submitted in the name of Erin Pizzey and my standing as the founder of the refuge movement was well known to everyone.

Women As Child-abusers

By this time I was working in Santa Fe, New Mexico on child abuse cases and against paedophiles. Here is where I discovered that there were just as many women paedophiles as there were men. Women go undetected, as usual. Working against paedophiles is a very dangerous business. I rescued a little British girl from a female paedophile in Britain while I was in New Mexico. It took three years of fighting against the English courts to rescue her and return her to her parents. When the official solicitor finally telephoned me and said I was right all along, and that the child had been abused, I asked him if he was going to prosecute the woman. He said no. Yet another woman got away and is still getting away with abusing children.

During all the years that I specialised in working with violent women and their children, I could never come to terms with the fear men had of violent women. I sat around dinner tables and in sitting rooms, listening to the feminist women abusing the men they lived with. I saw some women running what amounted to mini-concentration camps behind their front doors. I rarely ever saw a father stand up to a violent wife or lover. I hardly ever saw a father stop his wife abusing the children. They would come to me for help, but when faced with an angry and violent partner the men stayed quiet and tolerated the violence. Even now people laugh when a man says he has been abused. I don't find any sort of abuse to any living thing a laughing matter. I do feel that it is time that men recognised that women in the last 30 years have made many changes. They have become much more independent of men, but men have not yet made that step themselves.

It is depressing when working with men to find them running out of one violent relationship and then immediately looking for another woman to 'look after' them. Men have to get used to the idea that they can look after themselves. The younger generations of men seem to be aware of this male dependence upon women and can and do live by themselves.

When I was in Santa Fe a man came to see me who had lost his children and everything he owned because his little daughter had accused him of molesting her. I knew, from the moment he confessed that he was a womaniser, that he wasn't a child molester. After seeing the mother, who was a violent and manipulative narcissistic exhibitionist, I realised that she had instructed the child to name her father. I could see from the behaviour of the child that she had indeed been molested. Finally, after three months of work with her, she told me that the molester was a man who lived across the road. This man was a government official. When I took the evidence I had to the District Attorney's office he refused to target the case. A state trouper who also tried to get cases targeted me told me the DA was divorced on grounds of suspected child molestation so I had no chance anyway. I knocked on all the doors of the private houses I could find around his house and warned the neighbours. Many of them knew but were too frightened of him to do anything. When I confronted him he told me he was safe from prosecution because of his position and he would move his family to Alaska, where there was less chance of being convicted. He had, like so many violent and dangerous men, married a bride from the Philippines. She didn't dare say anything. Another little girl told me that her father, his new wife, and a neighbour raped her every Saturday afternoon during her access visit. I asked what hurt her the most about the abuse and she said 'her nails, they are very long and sharp in my...' and she pointed to her bottom. Those are the terrible details that confirm horrible truths.

Part of the problem with men is that they do not want to accept that women, and particularly the women they have loved, can be just as evil as men can. And yet we know that women perpetrate a high percentage of all child abuse. According to research from the US Department of Health and Human Services:

> Over 75 per cent of perpetrators of child maltreatment were parents, and an additional ten per cent were other relatives of the victim. It is estimated that over 80 per cent of all perpetrators were under age 40 and that almost two-thirds (62 per cent) were females.[4]

Susan Creighton's research for the NSPCC, published in 1992, found that natural mothers were recorded as the perpetrators in 30 per cent of physical injury cases, 37 per cent of emotional abuse cases, and 47 per cent of neglect cases.[5] This is where the core problem lies. Women who themselves have been unmothered and victims of dysfunctional family life cannot be asked to 'mother' their children as if all that is needed is a magic wand.

When I was in Canada for a six-week lecture tour in 1999, I was appalled at the fear I saw in men across this huge country. Sexual harassment cases at work mean that there are virtually no more office parties. I met a very fine professor who had been accused of sexual abuse of two of his students. He said living in Canada was like living in a totalitarian state. Indeed it was. I spoke to groups of men and women all over the country. Men there were already feeling the heavy hand of the state taking away their rights to their homes and their children. Men told stories of leaving the house to go to work and returning to find the woman had 'hoovered' the house, which means she had taken everything she could out of the house and disappeared with the children into a refuge. The distraught fathers were unable to find their wives and children because the refuges refused to disclose any information. In some cases, where the father is very violent, it is a necessary precaution, but I had never intended it to become routine so that many delinquent women could use this recourse against totally innocent men. For a woman, declaring your partner violent is a known fast-track to a divorce, and if that isn't sufficient women can now have recourse to what is called 'the silver bullet'. This means that she accuses her partner of sexually molesting the children. He is then cut off from his home and his family immediately. I was speaking to men's group in the West Country recently. Two police officers were at the meeting. They agreed, when I asked them about false sexual abuse, that they were indeed forced to take a father away from his family even when there was no evidence. In one case a woman had accused her child's father of having 'interfered' with her in the bath. She called the police and he was taken away immediately. Later he was released for lack of evidence. We should have a law that allows innocent victims of such allegations to sue their defamers.

The Neglect Of Abused Men

I find that men will not help each other the way women do. Men have had thousands of years of conditioning that enables them to work together very successfully, but when it comes to organising the same sort of help over their personal lives, they fall apart. I saw this happen when I tried to open a men's refuge almost immediately after I bought the main Chiswick building for the women's refuge. I had seen sufficient men who were horribly abused and needed somewhere to go. What offended me was that even though the Greater London Council was willing to give me an excellent building in North London, I could not get one single fund-raiser to help me raise money for the men.

Now we do have men's groups running in most countries, but as yet they have no funding, when millions of pounds are given to the women's refuges, some of which abuse the money they are given. We know we have huge problems with our young men. For the last 30 years they have been discriminated against in the media and in schools. These young men have been fed a diet of feminist rhetoric that assures them that they are 'rapists' and 'batterers'. Those were the placards that surrounded the Savoy Hotel when I was there for a luncheon and the launch of my book *Prone To Violence*.[6] This catalogued my work with violence -prone women and their children. I was used to the pickets because anywhere I spoke or appeared I was followed by these hate-filled women. I was aware that they held their secret conferences that excluded men all over the world. They have infiltrated most large institutions and the UN is filled with women who are determined to destroy the family and marriage as an institution. They want the family to be defined as women and children only. Men are to be sidelined. Their role as fathers is to be used as sperm banks and wallets. Fortunately those of us who believe in marriage and in the necessity of children having both biological parents in their lives, if at all possible, have time on our side. The women's movement is dying out as the elderly proponents now write books recanting their misspent youth and totter to their graves.

Notes

David G. Green

1 Gilder, G., *Wealth and Poverty*, London: Buchan & Enright, 1982, p. 130.

2 Wildavsky, A., quoted in Sykes, C., *A Nation of Victims*, New York: St Martin's Press, 1992, p. 13.

3 Elder, L., *Ten Things You Can't Say in America*, New York: St. Martin's Press, 2000, p. 23.

4 New York: Basic Books, 1981.

5 New York: William Morrow, 1984.

6 New York: William Morrow, 1990.

J.R. Shackleton and Peter Urwin

1 For detailed discussion, see Wright, R. and Ermisch, J. 'Gender discrimination in the British labour market: a reassessment', *Economic Journal*, Vol. 101, No. 406, 1991, pp. 508-22; Paci, P. and Joshi, H., 'Wage differentials between men and women', Department for Education and Employment, Research Series 71, 1996; Desai, T., Gregg, P., Steer, J. and Wadsworth, J., 'Gender and the labour market', in Gregg, P. and Wadsworth, J., *The State of Working Britain*, Manchester: Manchester University Press, 1999.

2 Harkness, S., 'The gender earnings gap: Evidence from the UK', *Fiscal Studies*, Vol. 17, No. 2, 1996, pp. 1-36.

3 Desai, *et al.*, 'Gender and the labour market', 1999.

4 Desai, *et al.*, 'Gender and the labour market', 1999.

5 Alpin, C. and Shackleton, J.R., 'Women in London's labour market', University of Westminster/London Chamber of Commerce and Industry, *Labour Market Briefing*, December 1997.

6 Desai, *et al.*, 'Gender and the labour market', 1999.

7 For a discussion see, for instance, Greenhalgh, C., Gregory, M. and Zissimos, B., 'The impact of trade, technological change and final demand on the skills structure of UK employment', paper presented at the

Royal Economic Society Conference, University of Warwick, April 1998; Machin, S. and van Reenan, J., 'Technology and changes in skill structure: evidence from seven OECD countries', paper presented at the Education and Employment Economics Group, London, January 1997.

8 Frost, M. and Spence, N., 'Employment changes in Central London in the 1980s', *The Geographical Journal,* Vol. 157, Part 2, 1991, pp. 125-35; Dex, S., 'Appropriate indicators of demand for labour markets segmented by gender', *Cambridge Journal of Economics*, Vol. 22, No. 1, 1998, pp. 19-38; Evans, P., 'Why has the female unemployment rate fallen so much in Britain?', Bank of England *Working Paper* 87, October 1998; Ward, C. and Dale, A., 'Geographical variation in female labour force participation: an application of multilevel modelling', *Regional Studies*, Vol. 26, No. 3, pp. 243-55.

9 Equal Opportunities Commission, *Briefings on Women and Men in Britain: The Labour Market,* Manchester: Equal Opportunities Commission, 1996.

10 Desai, *et al.*, 'Gender and the labour market', 1999.

11 Marks, J., London: CIVITAS, forthcoming.

12 Rigg, M., *Training in Britain: Individuals' Perspectives,* London: HMSO, 1989; Green, F., 'Sex discrimination in job-related training', *British Journal of Industrial Relations*, Vol. 29, No. 2, 1991, pp. 295-304.

13 Green, F., Machin, S. and Wilkinson, D., 'The determinants of workplace training', University of Leeds, School of Business Studies, *Discussion Paper* E96-01, 1996.

14 Taylor, P. E. and Urwin, P., 'Age and participation in vocational education and training', (mimeo) 2000.

15 Shackleton, J.R., 'Industrial relations reform in Britain since 1979', *Journal of Labor Research*, XIX, 3, 581-605, 1998.

16 Polachek, S.W. and Siebert, W.S., *The Economics of Earnings,* Cambridge: Cambridge University Press, 1993, p. 149.

17 Joshi, H., Paci, P. and Waldfogel, J., 'The wages of motherhood: better or worse?, *Cambridge Journal of Economics,* Vol. 23, 1999, pp. 543-64.

18 Rowthorn, R., 'Marriage and trust: some lessons from economics', *Cambridge Journal of Economics*, Vol. 23, 1999, pp. 661-91. He believes that women and children have lost out in other ways, however, and argues for a return to a divorce system based on the concept of fault.

19 See BBC News Website, 14 November 1999.

20 Nickell, S., 'Unemployment in Britain', in Gregg, P. and Wadsworth, J., *The State of Working Britain,* Manchester: Manchester University Press, 1999.

21 Evans, P., 'Why has the female unemployment rate fallen so much in Britain?', 1998.

22 *Labour Market Trends*, May 1999.

23 Hewitt, P., 'The place of part-time employment', in Meadows, P. (ed.), *Work Out - Or Work In?,* York: Joseph Rowntree Foundation, 1996.

24 *Labour Market Trends*, November 1997.

25 Sly, F., Thair, T. and Risden, A., 'Disability and the labour market: results from the winter 1998/99 Labour Force Survey', *Labour Market Trends,* September 1999, pp. 455-66.

26 Barmby, T., Ercolai, M. and Treble, J., 'Sickness absence in Great Britain: new quarterly and annual series from the GHS and LFS, 1971-1997', *Labour Market Trends,* August 1999, pp. 405-15.

27 Akerlof, G.A., 'Men without children', *The Economic Journal* Vol. 108, No. 447, 1998, pp. 287-309.

28 Beatty, C. and Fothergill, S., *The Detached Male Workforce,* Centre for Economic and Social Research, Sheffield Hallam University, 1999.

29 Taylor, P. E. and Urwin, P., 'Recent trends in the labour force participation of older people in the UK', *The Geneva Papers on Risk and Insurance,* Vol. 24, No. 4, 1999, pp. 551-79.

30 Disney, R., 'Why have older men stopped working?', in Gregg, P. and Wadsworth, J., *The State of Working Britain,* Manchester: Manchester University Press, 1999.

31 Guillemard, A-M., 'Travailleurs vieillessants et marche de travail en Europe', *Travail et Emploi,* Vol. 57, 1993, pp. 60-79.

32 Berthoud, R., *Young Caribbean Men and the Labour Market,* London: Joseph Rowntree Foundation, 1999.

Erin Pizzey

1 Brownmillar, S., *In Our Time: Memoir of a Revolution* The Dial Press, 1999.

2 Horowitz, M., *Hating Whitey and Other Progressive Causes*, Dallas: Spence Publishing, 1999.

3 Wiss, M. and Young, C., Cato Institute, police analysis paper, 'Feminist Jurisprudence': 'http://www.cato.org/pubs/pubs/pas/pa-256.html'.

4 US Department of Health and Human Services, 'Child Maltreatment 1997: Reports from the States to the National Child Abuse and Neglect Data System', Washington DC: UCCS Government Printing Office, 1999.

5 Creighton, S.J., *Child Abuse Trends in England and Wales 1988-1990*, London: NSPCC, 1992, p. 32.

6 Pizzey, E. and Shapiro, J., *Prone To Violence*, Hamlyn Paperbacks, 1982.